C000292660

Harry
and the Snowy Calf

By Ruth Chesney

Illustrated by Mary Weatherup

RITCHIE
John Ritchie Publishing

40 Beansburn, Kilmarnock, Scotland

ISBN-13: 978 1 912522 46 0

Copyright © 2019 by John Ritchie Ltd.
40 Beansburn, Kilmarnock, Scotland

www.ritchiechristianmedia.co.uk

All rights reserved. No part of this publication may be reproduced, stored in a retrievable system, or transmitted in any form or by any other means – electronic, mechanical, photocopy, recording or otherwise – without prior permission of the copyright owner.

Typeset by John Ritchie Ltd., Kilmarnock
Printed by Bell & Bain, Glasgow

This is Harry.

Harry lives on a farm with Daddy, Mummy, Little Sister Susie and Toby the dog.

One day Harry woke up and looked out of the window.
Everywhere was white!

"Susie, wake up! There's snow!" he shouted at the top of his voice. Little Sister Susie stood up in her cot and put her thumb in her mouth.

Harry got dressed. He put on his jeans, and his woolly jumper.
He found his socks and pulled them on, then ran downstairs
for his wellies and coat.

Outside, his breath made puffs of cloud in the air.

Toby the dog was also very excited about the snow. He and Harry ran around in circles, then they dug holes in the snow.

Daddy helped Harry make a snowman. They gave him a carrot for a nose. Toby stole the carrot. Naughty Toby!

After that, Harry and Daddy fed the hens...

Toby the dog...

...the sheep...

and Gladys the pig.

Then they went to feed Matilda the cow. She was getting very fat because she was going to have a calf.

Harry had been waiting for a long time for Matilda's calf to be born. He stroked her nose and gave her some extra hay.

The next morning Daddy was late for breakfast. At last, he poked his head around the door. "Hurry up, Harry," he said. "There's something exciting in the shed!"

Harry gobbled up the rest of his scrambled egg and toast, and took a big drink of milk.

Mummy helped him with his coat and wellies, then he followed Daddy across the yard.

"What is it, Daddy?" Harry asked.
Daddy smiled. "Wait and see."

They reached the shed and Daddy opened the door. Inside the pen was Matilda...

...and a pure white baby calf! "Moo!" said Matilda proudly.

"It's Matilda's baby!" exclaimed Harry. "What's its name?"
"You can name her," said Daddy.

Harry thought and thought. He scratched his head the way that Daddy did to help him think.

Finally - "Snowy!" he said. "She's called Snowy because she's all white like the snow outside."

Mummy and Susie came to see Snowy. "She's a beautiful calf,"
said Mummy.
"Moo-moo!" said Susie.

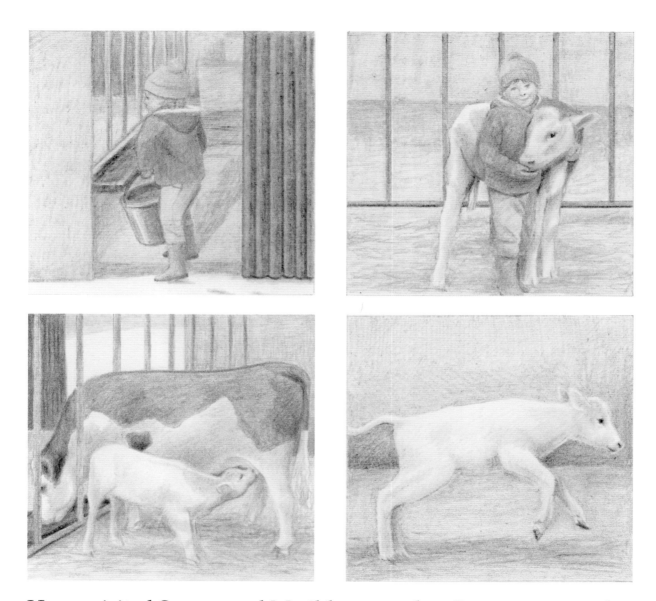

Harry visited Snowy and Matilda every day. Snowy grew and got stronger. Soon she was skipping around the pen.

Later that week, Harry went to help Daddy move Matilda and
Snowy to a bigger pen.

Snowy stepped out into the snow on her long, gangly legs.
Harry stared. Snowy looked dirty! She wasn't white like the snow
at all!
"Daddy, how did Snowy get so dirty?" asked Harry.

Daddy smiled. "She isn't dirty, Harry. She's the same colour as she always was. The pure white snow makes everything else look dirty."

"Even white things?" asked Harry.
"Yes," said Daddy. "You know, the Bible talks about the whiteness of snow."

"What does it say?" Harry asked.
"The Bible says that our sins are like scarlet - a big, bright red stain - and not just dirty white, the way Snowy looks compared with the snow."

(Isaiah 1:18)

"The Lord Jesus died on the cross so we could have our sins washed away. Now God can wash us and take away the stain to make us white. There's a verse in the Bible that says, 'Wash me, and I shall be whiter than snow.'"

(Psalm 51:7)

"Snow is very white," said Harry.
"It's the whitest thing there is. There's nothing in the world that is whiter than snow," replied Daddy.

"But it's very cold," said Harry, shivering.
Daddy laughed. "You're right, Harry! I think it's time we went inside to thaw out."

So Daddy and Harry went into the house and curled up by the fire with hot chocolate and a book.

And Snowy snuggled up beside Matilda in their new pen. In no time at all, she was fast asleep.